HOLLYHOCKS AND ROSES

Inspirational Insights for Your Life

BARBARA E. KOMPIK

1

Published by Createspace, a division of Amazon. 2018

Author: Barbara E. Kompik

Contact information:

Email: Barbara.e.kompik@gmail.com

Address: 7331 Oceana Drive, Hart, MI 49420

PREFACE

It can be lonely on this journey of life. It is a luxury to have someone to talk to while traveling the road. Someone to listen, to understand, and to empathize is invaluable. There is a friend that sticks closer than a sister or brother, one that has been abused emotionally and physically beyond recognition. One that hears my cries and comforts me, listens and interprets my groaning when I have no words to express the pain, and sings lullabies to me to calm my fears. My friendship with him is oh so very close - he knows and understands me better than I do myself. He takes my hand and leads me to quiet places and holds my heart in his hands so carefully as to not break it. He lets me crawl on his lap and rest in his arms and protects me as I sleep. I have known him for a very long time and he has never lied or betrayed me. His word has always been true. He has never once failed me. Whenever I call him, he is always home and answers me. He really cares about me and my feelings, and he always listens carefully to what I have to say. He always has an answer to my questions, and he is so wise. I haven't found anyone ever like him in my life. He is my refuge I run to when others are out to get me. He is my high tower where he keeps me safely from harm. He is my protector, always ready to fight for my dignity and well-being. He wipes every tear away, and teaches me new songs to sing in place of my sorrow and grief. He is always amazing and gives me more than I need. He loves and adores me. He whispers sweetness into my heart and soul. He frees me when I am bound up in confusion and pain. He's always there for me. I think I can do things myself, but really, I cannot live without him. He means everything to me. He is always with me and never leaves my side. He leads me to wisdom. ... His name is Jesus. He is my Savior and friend. We are forever friends. His blood runs through my veins and gives me life itself. I cannot exist without him. He is my very breath. I love him because he first loved me, and he has promised to love me into eternity. He is all and in all. He is forever.

FORWARD

We often believe that the cure for our half-hearted living out the truth of the

Gospel is to serve in our churches, to join the local evangelism challenge, and to

exercise what we understand to be the "spiritual disciplines" of Christian life. The

problem with this belief is that each of these 'cures' is focused on what we are

doing and not what Christ has done. The cure for our weak living is to recognize

our need for a Savior, to repent of our disbelief, and to rejoice that everything that

must be done has been done in Christ, and that all else is our futile attempt at self-

salvation.

- Dale Wayne Kompik II
  May, 1986 – December, 2017

HOLLYHOCKS AND ROSES

Inspirational Insights for Your Life

BARBARA E. KOMPIK

It is amazing the power that only one person can have as an effect on just

one other person that can change the world forever, and that is through

experience and creative thought.

If our hearts would touch but for a moment,

my life would be changed forever.

I don't think God ever takes our pain away except to place his soothing

Balm of Gilead on our wounds and waits for them to heal. What we envision

as "to be gone" remains a scar where once there was pain, healed, and sealed

into our hearts so that we never forget what it was like to have Jesus's power

heal us. Just like the scars on his hands and feet. they remain there as

evidence and a reminder of what he has brought us through, and we have

survived, and come alive and loving on the other side... I don't know if the

pain ever really disappears. But we learn to live with it as content as with an

old friend who knows all of our battle scars and yet remains our friend and

never leaves us. That is what it is like for me to have healed. Where once

were bloody wounds oozing with pain, there is an imprint of Jesus where he

came and left his healing mark. It is there to show others, in turn, that Jesus is alive and at work in my life. ... Try asking for the wounds to heal, rather than to take "your cup away from you." Just as Jesus prayed in Gethsemane before they killed him. God did not take his pain away, but he showed his presence dramatically with dark clouds where once there was sunshine, promising to deliver Jesus in 3 days from the dead....How can we expect anything less in our own lives? Go to your Gethsemane, take your closest friends, and earnestly pray for deliverance of this cup before you. God will transform you into a bright and holy light, just as he did for Jesus, glorifying his body and preparing him for heaven itself. Let yourself die unto yourself and allow God to raise you from the dead, resurrecting you into a bright and glorious light that shines with the truth of his miraculous power within you.

Our moments in time may be very different on this journey to wholeness

that we may miss the very moments that bring us hauntingly closer. It is

when the point of your journey and the point of my journey touch, connect,

and unite can we make each other's' journeys meaningful and our lives

changed.

You will touch my life in so many ways that will be innumerable and I yours. The most profound ways in which we are touched by spirit and soul are not the grandiose and spectacular. On the contrary. Our greatest moments of love, life, and learning are in the simple tears of pain shared and borne together until our spirits become one with each other and are healed. Those are the moments which we cherish forever.

Do not be deceived; there is only one thing that is forever in this life - the love between the Creator and the created. Everything else fades away as the flower to the sun.

Granted, unyielding grace: that is all I know of my life.

It has been many times I have wanted to give up and give in, and yet it is in those very times that I find the strength to carry on.

It is at the end of the rope that the knot of life begins.

It is within the simple things of life that I lose myself.

Everything in life matters, simply because you are

alive and breathing through this life.

You are; therefore, it is.

Let's face it; life is a mess.

And in each life a little dirt must fall.

When you reach the very pinnacle of worthlessness

do you begin to find true meaning in life.

It is in the reflection of the created that we see the truth of the Creator.....

Always reflect truth and you will find life itself.....

Truth and freedom walk hand in hand,

and nothing can separate them;

not even death itself.

THE CHAFFINCH NEST

How do you know your life matters for something? Because in the miniscule

molecules of your life resides the great vastness of people you know, lives

you've touched, and the difference your life made in theirs.

Jesus:

he is a relationship, personal,

and in your face and soul.

I could not do this scary and

demanding life without him.

He is right where I want

and need him - inside my heart.

I fall at the feet of my Jesus and cry out, do with me what you will and I will humbly serve you, for I WILL SEE that glorious hope and peace that is mine as your child. I have seen this light in near death and felt the peace and contentment that is ever present. I have felt him touch my face with his perfect though scarred hand, and felt myself transported under his wing on his lap. As I have said, I am putty in the Potter 's hands and will do the will of the Father even if it means death. I cannot ask for this cup to be taken from me, for I know that it will be used to help others, and then many of us shall shine together, even within this temporary life. God is good and he is good all the time.

Even though you may feel miserable and depressed, worthless and unloved, there are special qualities within you that ONLY YOU possesses. These qualities have been given to you to use for your benefit and the benefit of others as you pass through this life. They are to help and not to harm; they are to build up, not to break down. You must know what these qualities are in order to use them to their greatest potential ... and you alone must define them. No one else will define who you are to accentuate the best in you. And, too, others may be wrong about you and their perspectives may be skewed should you try to look to them to define you. It is important for you to know who YOU are, define YOURSELF, and discover all that YOU can be. You have been given a great gift - the gift of yourself. Use your gift wisely.

Are you in a battle in your life right now? Sometimes it feels so chaotic and overwhelming, draining all of the sap out of our veins. We get weary of difficulties darting our way like piercing arrows. We wonder if this turmoil is ever going to stop. The fact is Jesus says that we are in a battle within the mighty grips of war! We all live in war zones and we are standing in the middle of it all, fighting our way to stay standing, because getting knocked down by the enemy means death for sure.

So, Jesus says he TRAINS our hands and even our fingers for the battle, taking up our swords to fight on. Did you know that you are being shaped and trained as a mighty warrior just as Jesus himself is? And with him, we can take cover from whatever the enemy throws at us because he is our refuge and very tall tower where our enemy cannot reach us. We are protected under his wings because HE LOVES US SO MUCH!!!!!   If you are going through a battle today, get out your sword and FIGHT. For you are not alone. Jesus is in the battle with you, holding you up, not letting you fall, and protecting you with his shield.

Take courage for he's got your back. Fight on, never give up, and know that Jesus will fight to the end until your enemies will stop fighting you.

We who have unbearable pain find ourselves alone much of our lives until we are healed. And I believe that is exactly our pain's purpose - so that we can be alone with Jesus, our comforter and healer and pray our heart out to him. It is difficult for people to hang in there with our pain with us. They get tired easily, and abandon us just like the disciples did with Jesus the night before he died. They didn't have the emotional or physical stamina just to stay awake and support Jesus in his last hours. So it is with us. Jesus gives us a painful task to do, to bear up under the weight of our pain alone. We cannot expect anyone else to be there for us; we must carry our cross alone, just as Jesus did. In that way we are drawn to the Father to beg his mercy upon us, praying for relief from the pain, just as Jesus did with God, his father.

God did not take Jesus's pain and burden away until he had walked with him through his death on the cross. He helped him through the excruciating pain. Jesus also experienced abandonment from his own father as God could not look upon the sin that Jesus was bearing. But when Jesus finally died unto himself and gave up his spirit to God, did God bring him back to life and healed his wounds. Oh, he had scars where they abused him, but they were to remind us of his suffering and just what he went through to purchase each one of us that accept his gift of love. God then glorified Jesus with a new body that shone as bright as the sun. He finally gave Jesus his rightful place next to God on his throne. I see the same thing happening in my life as Jesus lived his. What an honor to be called to walk in Jesus's shoes, carry the pain, and draw close to him. Because even in this life he gives us the light of himself, so that we, too, can shine for his glory, and when our lives are finished here, that we will be standing in the brilliant light and glory of God. Amazing. What an awesome God we serve.

Are you listening? Listen to Jesus.

But the thing is, you must quiet your

heart and soul to hear him,

for he does not shout.

He whispers.

Listen.

AUTHOR BIOGRAPHY

Barbara E. Kompik

Barbara lives on the coast of Lake Michigan with her husband. She has three children, whom she loves dearly. Her passion is writing her heart onto the pages of clean sheets of computer screen and creating something beautiful for others to enjoy.

She has eleven years of higher education behind her in Psychology, Social Work, Business and Creative Writing, having gone back to work on finishing her degree at age 45.

Barbara loves to travel to speak to audiences to share her hope and healing from abuse she endured as a child, and the grief she experienced in losing her 31 year old son at Christmastime, 2017.

In her spare time, Barbara works with her husband to renovate their 100+ year old country home on three acres, filled with 400+ year old trees and new gardens of flowers they have planted. It is her dream to sit out on their wrap around porch and enjoy visiting with friends from around the world.

A NOTE FROM THE AUTHOR

After what has been a very challenging and painful few years, I can finally say that I am very content with my life......doing dishes every morning, cleaning the house and decorating it, cooking, making the bed, stoking the fire, calling my kids, writing, listening to my music, rocking, staying in touch with friends I love, working on this old run down house, taking pictures, and sharing things that Jesus shares with me with you. It hasn't always been that way. I'm enjoying the simple and unrushed life.

It's good.

Made in the USA
Lexington, KY
03 August 2019